48012

AZTEC & MAYAN MYTHS

by David West

illustrated by Mike Taylor

BOOK HOUSE

Designed and produced by
David West Children's Books
7 Princeton Court
55 Felsham Road
London SW15 1AZ

Editor: Dominique Crowley

Photo credits:
Page 4, Jack Poe
Page 5, Skip Hunt

First published in 2006 by **Book House,**
an imprint of **The Salariya Book Company Ltd**
25 Marlborough Place, Brighton BN1 1UB

Please visit the Salariya Book Company at:
www.salariya.com

HB ISBN 1 905087 69 1
PB ISBN 1 905087 70 5

Visit our website at **www.book-house.co.uk**
for free electronic versions of:
You Wouldn't Want to Be an Egyptian Mummy!
You Wouldn't Want to Be a Roman Gladiator!
Avoid joining Shackleton's Polar Expedition!

A catalogue record for this book is available from the British Library.
Printed on paper from sustainable forests.

Manufactured in China.

CONTENTS

ANCIENT CIVILISATIONS

Mesoamerica, the name used to describe Mexico and Central America, has a rich history of ancient cultures and civilisations. The Toltecs were one of the earliest cultures, and many of their gods influenced the later civilisations of the Maya and the Aztecs.

RELIGION AND MYTHOLOGY

Religion and mythology were central to the lives of these ancient cultures. Myths and stories about gods helped them make sense of the world. The Aztecs, for example, believed that the Spanish explorer Hernan Cortés, who conquered them, was not a foreign enemy, but the god Quetzalcóatl returning to Earth.

Aztecs believed that the world was created five times. On the calendar above, the four rectangles around the central sun god represent the four previous creations of life on Earth.

This Mayan statue of a tlachtli player looks out over the jungle. Tlachtli was a sacred ball game played by Mesoamericans. In the game, two teams tried to bounce a rubber ball through a stone hoop high up on a wall.

A sculptured reptile sticks out from Teotihuacán's Temple of Quetzalcóatl (right). Often, these sculptures were painted in bright colours, and the eyes were made of volcanic glass.

HEAVENS ABOVE

Mesoamerican cultures believed that there was not just one heaven, but many. One way to reach these heavens was by human sacrifice. People were willing to be sacrificed because they hoped that they would go to heaven. It was an agonising way to die, and the heart was often ripped out of the body. The main reasons people were sacrificed was to honour the gods, and to ensure healthy crops. Their idea of Hell was a place of emptiness and boredom.

Sacrifice was common to all the Mesoamerican cultures. Some myths are stories that give reasons for these killings.

THREE MESOAMERICAN MYTHS

Mesoamerica was an area that included Mexico and Central America, before parts of it were taken over in the sixteenth century by Europeans. It was home to the Toltec, Olmec, Aztec and Mayan civilisations. By reading their myths, we can learn a lot about these cultures.

QUETZALCÓATL AND TEZCATLIPOCA CREATE THE WORLD (AZTEC)

The Aztecs believed that the world was created five times. The gods kept destroying the world because they were not pleased with what they had made. Each time they re-created it, they tried to make the world better. This myth is the story of the fifth and final, creation. It tells what happened when the two gods, Quetzalcóatl and Tezcatlipoca, destroyed the goddess Tlatecuhtli and used her body to create the world for the last time.

Quetzalcóatl
A very important god in Aztec mythology, this feathered snake shares his name with a famous king from the Toltec civilisation. He is a kind god. In human form, he has a grey beard.

Tezcatlipoca
The god of warriors, the night-sky and the thunderbolt, he is also known as the 'Smoking Mirror' because he carries a magic mirror. This mirror reveals people's thoughts.

Tlatecuhtli
Sometimes known as the 'Earth Monster', this goddess lives in water. Some say that 20,000 people every year were sacrificed by the Aztecs to please her.

CREATION OF THE SUN, MOON, AND PEOPLE (AZTEC)

Creation stories help people understand who they are and where they came from. They provide important links to a long-lost past, especially to the way of life of their ancestors. This creation story helped Aztecs imagine how the world might have begun. It contains information about the gods, sacrifice, and religion, and shows that people cannot be judged by their appearance.

Tecciztécatl
This god of snails is proud and attractive. Later, he becomes the god of the moon.

Nanautzin
Known as the 'Scabby One', Nanautzin is small, quiet and thoughtful. He always wears old clothes.

Mictlantecuhtli
This god of the dead lives in the Underworld, a place where evil spirits go after death.

THE HERO TWINS (MAYA)

According to the Popol Vuh and Mayan mythology, there were two sets of hero twins. Both enjoyed the sacred ball game tlachtli, but they played it so noisily that they upset the gods. The Lords of the Underworld challenged them to a game, with a fatal outcome.

Hun Hunahpu
Vucub Hunahpu's twin, this forefather god has four sons.

Vucub Hunahpu
The other hero twin, he has neither a wife nor children.

Hun Came
One of two Kings of Death. He rules the Underworld (Xibalba).

Vucub Came
Other lord of the Underworld. His name means 'Seven Death'.

Hunahpu
Son of Hun Hunahpu, and the hero twin brother of Xbalanque.

Xbalanque
Clever hero twin. He uses great skill when playing ball in the Underworld.

QUETZALCÓATL AND TEZCATLIPOCA CREATE THE WORLD
FROM THE AZTEC PEOPLE

HUH! WHAT IS THAT?

TWO OF THE MANY GODS HAVE BEEN CREATING PARTS OF THE WORLD. QUETZALCÓATL, THE FEATHERED SERPENT GOD, AND TEZCATLIPOCA, GOD OF THE SMOKING MIRROR, LOOK DOWN ON THE WATER FROM THE SKY.

IT IS TLATECUHTLI, THE GIANT WATER GODDESS. AND SHE'S EATING EVERYTHING WE HAVE CREATED!

THE GODDESS EATS WHILE THE TWO GODS DECIDE WHAT TO DO...

YES, CHANGE INTO A SNAKE. SNAKES FIGHT BETTER IN WATER...

LET US JOIN FORCES TO RID OURSELVES OF THIS MONSTER.

THEY DIVE OUT OF THE CLOUDS...

...INTO THE OCEAN...

...AND SNEAK UP TO TLATECUHTLI FROM BELOW.

9

QUETZALCÓATL GRABS THE GODDESS BY THE ARMS...

...TEZCATLIPOCA GRABS HER BY THE LEGS...

...BEFORE SHE CAN DEFEND HERSELF, TLATECUHTLI IS PULLED APART...

...AND THE BROKEN PIECES OF HER BODY BECOME THE EARTH.

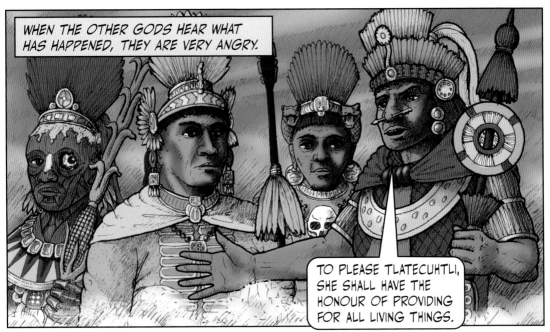

WHEN THE OTHER GODS HEAR WHAT HAS HAPPENED, THEY ARE VERY ANGRY.

TO PLEASE TLATECUHTLI, SHE SHALL HAVE THE HONOUR OF PROVIDING FOR ALL LIVING THINGS.

FROM HER HAIR, THEY CREATE TREES, GRASS AND FLOWERS...

...CAVES, FOUNTAINS AND WELLS FROM HER EYES...

...RIVERS FROM HER MOUTH...

...AND MOUNTAINS FROM HER SHOULDERS.

BUT TLATECUHTLI IS UNHAPPY. WHEN PEOPLE APPEAR IN THE WORLD, THEY CAN HEAR HER CRYING IN THE NIGHT.

AAAIIEEE

THEY BELIEVE SHE IS THIRSTY FOR THEIR BLOOD.

SHE WILL NOT PROVIDE FOOD FROM THE SOIL UNTIL SHE DRINKS BLOOD!

AND SO...

...SHE WHO GIVES US LIFE...

DEMANDS HUMAN LIVES TO PROVIDE FOR HER!

SO IT HAS ALWAYS BEEN, SO IT WILL BE FOREVER.

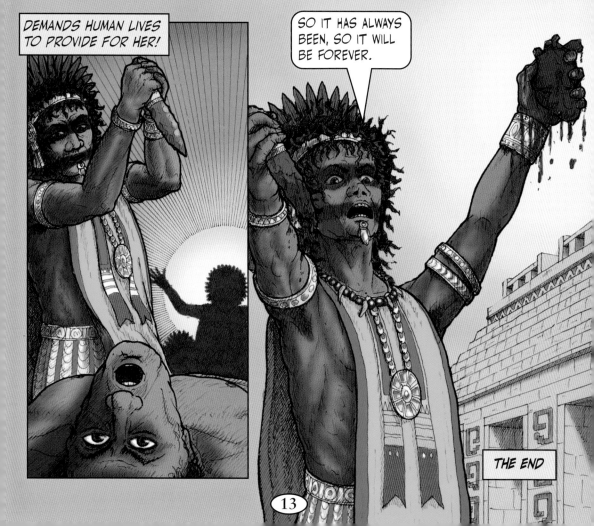

THE END

13

THE CREATION OF THE SUN, MOON AND PEOPLE

FROM THE AZTEC PEOPLE

THE GODS' FOURTH ATTEMPT AT CREATING EARTH AND PEOPLE HAD BEEN DESTROYED AND THE WORLD IS IN TOTAL DARKNESS. THE GODS MEET TO DECIDE WHAT TO DO NEXT.

EACH TIME A CREATION IS DESTROYED, THE SUN IS DESTROYED.

ONE OF THE GODS MUST JUMP INTO THE FIRE TO CREATE A NEW SUN. WHO AMONG YOU WILL SACRIFICE YOURSELF?

TWO GODS STEP FORWARD. ONE IS RICH AND HANDSOME...

MY NAME IS TECCIZTÉCATL. I WILL JUMP INTO THE FLAMES AND BECOME THE MOST BEAUTIFUL AND BRILLIANT SUN.

THE OTHER IS POOR, UGLY AND COVERED IN SORES.

I AM NANAUTZIN. I HAVE NOTHING TO OFFER YOU EXCEPT MY POOR BODY. BUT I WILL BECOME THE SUN IF YOU SO CHOOSE.

THE HANDSOME GOD IS GIVEN THE HONOUR OF SACRIFICING HIMSELF. A FIRE IS PREPARED.

THE HANDSOME GOD IS ASHAMED OF HIS COWARDICE AND JUMPS INTO THE DYING FLAMES OF THE FIRE.

AT THIS POINT, A JAGUAR ALSO JUMPS INTO THE ASHES OF THE DYING FIRE.

WHEN IT LEAPS OUT, IT IS COVERED IN SOOTY PRINTS. THIS IS HOW THIS NOBLE BEAST GOT ITS MARKINGS.

THE GODS WATCH AND WAIT...

...GRADUALLY, A GLOW APPEARS ON THE HORIZON...

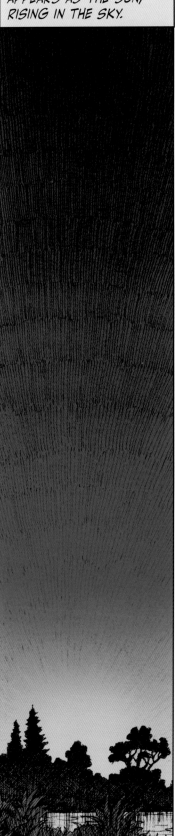

...SLOWLY, NANAUTZIN APPEARS AS THE SUN, RISING IN THE SKY.

BUT THERE IS SOMETHING NOT QUITE RIGHT...

...TECCIZTÉCATL, THE MOON, IS FOLLOWING THE SUN CLOSELY. HE IS SHINING JUST AS BRIGHTLY.

HOW DARE TECCIZTÉCATL DO THIS? HE DOES NOT DESERVE TO SHINE SO MUCH! ARRGGH!

THE ANGRY GODS SLAP HIM IN THE FACE WITH A RABBIT...

SCHLAPPP

...AND THAT IS HOW THE MOON GOT ITS MARKINGS.

AFTER THE CREATION OF THE FIFTH SUN, QUETZALCÓATL DECIDED IT WAS TIME TO CREATE PEOPLE.

I SHALL GO TO THE UNDERWORLD AND ASK FOR THE BONES OF DEAD HUMANS FROM THE EARLIER CREATIONS.

BE WARY OF MICTLANTECUHTLI.*
HE IS NOT TO BE TRUSTED.

*LORD OF THE DEAD

MICTLANTECUHTLI GIVES QUETZALCÓATL A LARGE BAG FILLED WITH THE BONES OF DEAD PEOPLE.

I AM SURE I WILL SEE THEM AGAIN SOON ENOUGH. HA HA HA!

REMEMBERING THAT MICTLANTECUHTLI WAS NOT TO BE TRUSTED, QUETZALCÓATL HURRIES AWAY.

IN HIS HASTE, HE SLIPS AND DROPS THE BAG...

...BREAKING ALL THE BONES INTO SMALLER PIECES.

KERSMACK

LATER, ON EARTH, QUETZALCÓATL MIXES HIS BLOOD WITH THE BROKEN BONES TO MAKE THE PEOPLE OF THE FIFTH CREATION. ALL THE PIECES OF BONES ARE DIFFERENT SIZES. THIS IS WHY PEOPLE ARE DIFFERENT HEIGHTS AND SHAPES.

THE END

THE HERO TWINS
FROM THE MAYAN PEOPLE

THE EARTH SHAKES AS THE BROTHERS HUN HUNAHPU AND VUCUB HUNAHPU PLAY THE
BALL GAME, TLACHTLI WITH HUN HUNAHPU'S SONS, HUN BATZ AND HUN CHOUEN.

HUN CAME AND VUCUB CAME ARE THE SUPREME GODS OF XIBALBA (THE UNDERWORLD). THEY ARE ANGRY.

A MEETING IS CALLED. ALL THE GODS OF XIBALBA ARE PRESENT.

WHAT IS THAT TERRIBLE NOISE? IS IT THOSE BROTHERS PLAYING TLACHTLI AGAIN? HAVE THEY NO RESPECT FOR US?

IT IS DECIDED! WE WILL CALL THE BROTHERS TO US. THEY WILL FAIL THE TASKS WE SET FOR THEM. THEN WE WILL KILL THEM AS A SACRIFICE.

ASK THEM TO BRING THEIR TLACHTLI KIT. WE WILL WANT IT AFTER THEY ARE KILLED. SEND FOR THE OWL MESSENGERS.

THE OWL MESSENGERS, CHABI-TUCUR, HURACÁN-TUCUR, CAQUIX-TUCUR AND HOLOM-TUCUR GIVE THE MESSAGE TO HUN HUNAHPU AND VUCUB HUNAHPU.

THE TWO BROTHERS DECIDE TO HIDE THEIR KIT IN THE RAFTERS OF THEIR HOUSE.

THE GODS OF XIBALBA DEMAND THAT YOU COME TO THEM WITH YOUR TLACHTLI KIT.

LET US GO HOME TO SAY FAREWELL TO OUR FAMILY. THEN WE WILL COME WITH YOU.

THEY WILL KILL YOU, MY SONS.

DO NOT WORRY, MOTHER. SEE, WE LEAVE OUR KIT SO THAT WE CAN PLAY WHEN WE RETURN.

SOON, THEY ARE DESCENDING THE STEEP STEPS DOWN INTO THE UNDERWORLD.

THEY CROSS MANY RIVERS AND PASS THROUGH MANY THORNY REGIONS WITHOUT HURTING THEMSELVES.

NEXT, THEY WALK THROUGH A RIVER OF BLOOD.

DON'T DRINK FROM IT! IT RUNS WITH BLOOD.

FINALLY, THEY COME TO A CROSSROAD.

I AM THE ROAD YOU MUST TAKE.

THE TWO BROTHERS FAIL THE FIRST TEST. THEY MISTAKE TWO WOODEN FIGURES FOR THE GODS.

HOW ARE YOU HUN CAME?
HOW ARE YOU VUCUB CAME?

NEXT, THE GODS TRICK THE BROTHERS INTO SITTING ON A HOT BENCH. THEY FAIL THE SECOND TEST.

HA HA! TOMORROW, WE WILL PLAY A GAME OF TLACHTLI. TONIGHT, YOU WILL SPEND THE NIGHT IN THE HOUSE OF GLOOM. HERE ARE TWO CIGARS AND PINE STICKS FOR LIGHT. YOU MUST RETURN THEM AS GOOD AS NEW IN THE MORNING.

HUN HUNAHPU AND VUCUB HUNAHPU SMOKE THE CIGARS AND BURN THE PINE STICKS FOR LIGHT.

IN THE MORNING, THE TWO BROTHERS COULD NOT RETURN THE CIGARS AND THE PINE STICKS AS GOOD AS NEW. THEY HAD FAILED THE THIRD TEST.

TODAY, YOU WILL DIE. YOU SHALL BE SACRIFICED!

THAT SAME DAY, THE BROTHERS ARE SACRIFICED. THEIR BODIES ARE BURIED UNDER THE TLACHTLI COURT IN XIBALBA.

THE HEAD OF HUN HUNAHPU IS CUT-OFF AND PLACED AMONG THE BRANCHES OF A CALABASH TREE THAT HAS NEVER BLOSSOMED.

TO EVERYONE'S SURPRISE, THE TREE STARTS TO BEAR FRUIT. PEOPLE COME FROM ALL AROUND TO SEE IT. BUT THEY ARE FORBIDDEN BY THE LORDS TO PICK THE FRUIT.

ONE DAY, XQUIC, THE DAUGHTER OF LORD CUCHUMAQUIC, COMES TO SEE THE TREE.

I WONDER WHAT WILL HAPPEN IF I PICK SOME OF THE FRUIT?

THE SKULL OF HUN HUNAHPU APPEARS AND SPEAKS TO THE GIRL. AS SHE LIFTS UP HER HAND, HE SPITS INTO IT, MAKING HER PREGNANT WITH TWINS.

IF YOU WANT ONE, STRETCH OUT YOUR HAND. I WILL SPIT INTO IT, AND YOU WILL BE THE MOTHER OF MY CHILDREN.

WHEN IT IS DISCOVERED THAT XQUIC IS PREGNANT, HER FATHER TAKES THE MATTER TO HUN CAME AND VUCUB CAME.

VERY WELL. THE FOUR OWLS WILL TAKE HER TO BE SACRIFICED. THEY SHALL RETURN WITH HER HEART IN A GOURD.

THE OWLS SET OFF CARRYING A GOURD, A KNIFE AND THE PREGNANT XQUIC.

OH! PLEASE! YOU CANNOT KILL ME. I AM PREGNANT WITH THE SONS OF HUN HUNAHPU.

WE DO NOT WANT TO KILL YOU, BUT WHAT CAN WE DO?

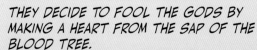

THEY DECIDE TO FOOL THE GODS BY MAKING A HEART FROM THE SAP OF THE BLOOD TREE.

PLACE THE 'HEART' IN THE GOURD AND ADD SOME MORE RED SAP FOR BLOOD.

WE WILL RETURN TO YOU WHEN WE HAVE DELIVERED THIS.

THEY SHOW THE GODS OF XIBALBA THE FAKE HEART.

IT IS DONE. THROW IT ON THE FIRE!

THE GODS HAD BEEN TRICKED! THE FOUR OWLS LEAVE XIBALBA TO BECOME THE GIRL'S SERVANTS.

XQUIC FINDS HUN HUNAHPU'S WIFE AND CHILDREN, HUN BATZ AND HUN CHOUEN, AND GIVES BIRTH TO THE HERO TWINS, HUNAHPU AND XBALANQUE.

HUN BATZ AND HUN CHOUEN BECOME JEALOUS OF THE TWINS. EVENTUALLY, THEY ARE TURNED INTO MONKEYS BY HUNAHPU AND XBALANQUE. BUT THAT IS ANOTHER STORY...

THE TWINS BECOME GREAT BLOWPIPE HUNTERS. BUT THEY DON'T DO ANYTHING TO HELP THEIR MOTHER OR GRANDMOTHER.

WHY DON'T YOU TWO FARM SOME LAND SO THAT WE MIGHT HAVE VEGETABLES TO EAT?

TO PLEASE THEIR MOTHER AND GRANDMOTHER, THE TWINS CLEAR A PATCH OF JUNGLE FOR FARMLAND.

THEY COME BACK THE NEXT DAY, TO FIND THAT THE FIELD LOOKS LIKE A JUNGLE AGAIN.

THEY CLEAR THE LAND AGAIN. BUT THIS TIME, THEY HIDE WHEN THEY HAVE FINISHED AND WAIT FOR DARKNESS.

WHO HAS DONE THIS?

I THINK IT WAS PROBABLY THE ANIMALS OF THE JUNGLE.

AT MIDNIGHT, THE ANIMALS APPEAR IN THE AREA THAT THE TWINS HAVE CLEARED. THEY USE MAGIC TO MAKE THE TREES AND OTHER PLANTS GROW BACK AGAIN.

THE TWINS RUSH OUT TO GRAB THE ANIMALS, BUT MOST OF THEM ARE TOO QUICK. THEY CATCH THE TAILS OF RABBITS AND DEER, BUT THEY BREAK FREE, LEAVING THEIR TAILS IN THE TWINS' HANDS. THIS IS WHY DEER AND RABBITS HAVE SHORT TAILS.

EVENTUALLY, THEY CATCH A RAT. IT REFUSES TO TALK TO THEM SO THEY HOLD ITS TAIL OVER A FIRE. THIS IS WHY RATS TAILS ARE WITHOUT HAIR.

AAARGH! DON'T HURT ME!! YOU TWO AREN'T MEANT TO BE FARMERS. GIVE ME SOME FOOD, AND I WILL TELL YOU A SECRET.

THE RAT TELLS THEM THAT THEIR FATHER AND UNCLE WERE GREAT TLACHTLI PLAYERS. HE SAYS THAT THE TWINS COULD BE GREAT PLAYERS, TOO, INSTEAD OF BEING FARMERS!

ALL YOU NEED IS SOME GOOD KIT. AND I KNOW WHERE YOUR DAD AND UNCLE HID IT.

THE RAT TAKES THEM TO THEIR GRANDMOTHER'S HOUSE AND POINTS TO THE RAFTERS.

THE TWINS TELL THEIR GRANDMOTHER TO GO OUT TO GET SOME WATER IN A JUG. THEY ASK A MOSQUITO TO MAKE A HOLE IN THE JUG. THEN THEY SEND THEIR MOTHER OUT TO FIND OUT WHY THEIR GRANDMOTHER IS TAKING SO LONG.

QUICK BROTHER! WHILE WE ARE ALONE, GET THE KIT BEFORE THEY RETURN.

WE WILL HIDE IT IN THE FIELDS FOR NOW.

FOOD?

THE RAT GNAWS THROUGH THE ROPE AND THE SACK FALLS TO THE GROUND.

THE NEXT DAY, THE TWINS CLEAR THE TLACHTLI COURT THAT THEIR FATHER AND UNCLE PLAYED ON...

...AND BEGIN TO PLAY BALL...

WHO ARE THEY WHO SHOW NO RESPECT BY MAKING SUCH NOISE? SEND FOR THEM. TELL THEM WE WISH TO PLAY TLACHTLI WITH THEM.

WHEN THE TWINS GET THE MESSAGE FROM THE GODS OF XIBALBA, THEY SAY GOODBYE TO THEIR MOTHER AND GRANDMOTHER.

THEY WILL KILL YOU LIKE THEY KILLED YOUR FATHER AND UNCLE.

DO NOT WORRY. WE WILL SUCCEED WHERE OUR FATHER AND UNCLE FAILED.

SOON THEY ARE DESCENDING THE STAIRS TO XIBALBA.

HAVING CROSSED MANY RAVINES, THEY COME TO THE RIVER OF BLOOD, WHERE THE PEOPLE OF XIBALBA HOPE THEY WILL FAIL.

DO NOT TOUCH THE WATER, BROTHER. DO AS I DO AND USE YOUR BLOWPIPE.

WHEN THEY REACH THE CROSSWAY, HUNAHPU PLUCKS A HAIR FROM HIS LEG TO MAKE A MOSQUITO.

XAN, GO AND STING THE GODS SO THAT WE WILL HEAR THEIR NAMES.

WHEN XAN STINGS THE WOODEN STATUES, THEY MAKE NO SOUND.

OUCH!

WHAT IS IT, HUN CAME?

ARG!

WHAT IS IT, VUCUB CAME?

AH!

OW!

WHAT IS IT, AHALPUH?

OW!

YOW!

THIS IS HOW THE TWINS LEARN ALL THE NAMES OF THE GODS OF XIBALBA.

33

THE TWINS IGNORE THE WOODEN STATUES AND GREET ALL THE GODS BY THEIR NAMES.

PLEASE TAKE A SEAT.

THEY DO NOT FALL FOR THE SECOND TRICK EITHER. THE LORDS OF XIBALBA ARE ANGRY, BUT THEY ARE SURE THAT THEY WILL FOOL THE BROTHERS IN THE NEXT TEST.

NOT ON THAT COOKING GRIDDLE WE WON'T.

THE PAIR ARE GIVEN CIGARS AND LIGHTED PINES AND ARE TOLD TO RETURN THEM IN THE MORNING.

TAKE THESE TO THE HOUSE OF GLOOM.

PUT OUT THE FIRE. WE CAN USE THIS MACAW FEATHER AS A FLAME. PUT A FIREFLY ON THE END OF YOUR CIGAR. THEY WILL THINK IT IS LIT UP.

FROM OUTSIDE, THE GUARDS ONLY SEE WHAT THE TWINS WISH THEM TO SEE.

WHAT TRICKERY IS THIS? NOW WE SHALL HAVE TO BEAT YOU AT BALL.

IN THE MORNING, THE CIGARS AND PINES ARE RETURNED WHOLE.

AND SO, THE TWINS PLAY TLACHTLI AGAINST THE LORDS OF XIBALBA, AND BEAT THEM BY SENDING THE BOUNCING BALL SOARING THROUGH THE STONE CIRCLE.

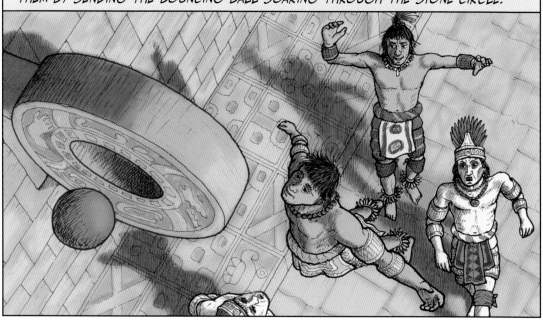

THE GODS ARE ANGRY AND GIVE THE TWINS ANOTHER SEEMINGLY IMPOSSIBLE TASK.

YOU SHALL SPEND THE NIGHT IN THE HOUSE OF KNIVES.

IN THE MORNING, YOU ARE TO GIVE US FLOWERS.

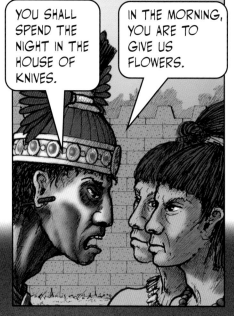

AT NIGHT, THE GUARDS DO NOT NOTICE THE ANTS STEALING THE FLOWERS IN FRONT OF THEM.

THE TWINS CONVINCE THE KNIVES THAT THEY SHOULD NOT CUT THE FLESH OF PEOPLE.

THE TWINS THEN CALL THE ANTS TO THEM.

GO, ZOMPOPOS, AND CUT THE FLOWERS FOR US.

IN THE MORNING, THE TWINS PRESENT THE GODS WITH BUNCHES OF FLOWERS.

WHO ARE THESE PEOPLE? THEY HAVE TRICKED US AGAIN!

THE GODS PLAY WITH THEM AGAIN. THEY HOPE TO DEFEAT THE TWINS. SEVERAL GAMES ARE PLAYED, BUT ALL OF THEM END IN A TIE.

EVERY NIGHT, FOR THREE NIGHTS THE TWINS ARE TESTED...

...IN THE HOUSE OF COLD, THEY BUILD A FIRE TO KEEP WARM...

...IN THE HOUSE OF JAGUARS, THEY FEED THE ANIMALS BONES...

...IN THE HOUSE OF FIRE, THEY ARE UNHARMED - ONLY THE WOOD BURNS.

THEN THEY ARE SENT TO THE HOUSE OF CAMAZOTZ, WHICH IS FULL OF BATS. BUT THE BROTHERS SLEEP INSIDE THEIR BLOWPIPES.

IS IT DAWN YET, BROTHER?

I WILL SEE...

IT'S...

SLASHHHH

AT DAWN, XBALANQUE FINDS HIS BROTHER'S DECAPITATED BODY. HE CALLS ALL THE ANIMALS TO BRING THEIR FOOD TO HIM.

AH, COATI. I WILL NEED YOUR SQUASH.

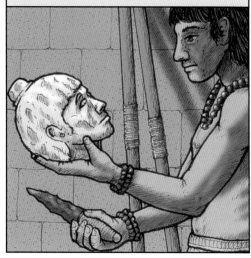

HE CARVES THE SQUASH TO LOOK LIKE THE HEAD OF HIS BROTHER.

XBALANQUE CALLS A RABBIT TO HIM.

HIDE NEAR THE TREE. WHEN YOU SEE THE BALL COMING NEAR, RUN OUT INTO THE FOREST AS FAST AS YOU CAN.

THE GODS OF XIBALBA ARE SURE THEY WILL WIN. IN THIS FINAL GAME, THEY DECIDE TO PLAY WITH THE TWIN'S HEAD AS THE BALL.

XBALANQUE BOUNCES THE HEAD TOWARD THE TREE.

AS THE HEAD FALLS CLOSE TO THE RABBIT, HE JUMPS OUT AND HOPS INTO THE FOREST.

THERE IT GOES.

XBALANQUE REPLACES THE HEAD WITH THE SQUASH. HE HANDS HUNAHPU THE HEAD, AND HE PUTS IT BACK ONTO HIS NECK.

WATCH THIS!

THE GODS RETURN FROM THE FOREST AND SEE THE 'HEAD' ON THE GROUND.

THERE IT IS!

HUH?

HAHA! HO! HO!

ONCE AGAIN, THE GODS OF XIBALBA HAVE BEEN OUTWITTED.

THE GODS OF XIBALBA CANNOT KILL THE TWINS, EVEN WITH ALL THEIR TRICKERY. BUT THE TWINS KNOW THEY WILL NEVER BE FREE UNLESS THEY DIE. THEY CALL THE WISE MEN TO THEM.

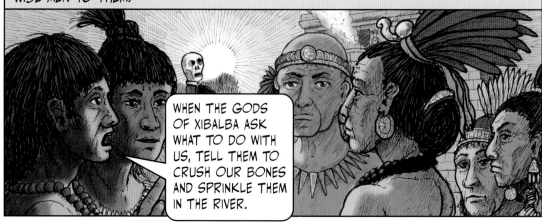

WHEN THE GODS OF XIBALBA ASK WHAT TO DO WITH US, TELL THEM TO CRUSH OUR BONES AND SPRINKLE THEM IN THE RIVER.

WHEN THE LORDS OF XIBALBA CALL THE TWINS TO A NEW GAME, THE TWINS KNOW IT IS A TRICK...

SEE THIS FIRE? WE BET YOU CAN'T JUMP OVER IT FOUR TIMES.

THEY BOTH JUMP INTO THE FIRE AND DIE.

THE LORDS OF XIBALBA ARE DELIGHTED THAT THE TWINS ARE FINALLY DEAD.

TELL US, WISE MEN, WHAT SHALL WE DO WITH THEIR BONES?

GRIND THEM UP AND THROW THEM INTO THE RIVER SO THAT THEY ARE SCATTERED AND LOST FOREVER.

THE LORDS DO AS THE WISE MEN SUGGEST.

AS IT HAPPENS, THIS IS THE ONLY WAY THE TWINS COULD BE BROUGHT BACK TO LIFE. FIRST AS CATFISH...

...THEN AS MEN. BUT NOBODY RECOGNISES THEM BECAUSE THEY LOOK LIKE BEGGARS.

THEY TRAVEL AROUND XIBALBA, ENTERTAINING THE PEOPLE WITH THEIR SONGS, DANCES AND THEIR MAGIC. THEY CAN BURN A HOUSE DOWN AND THEN REBUILD IT IN A MOMENT. THEY CAN ALSO CHOP A MAN INTO PIECES AND THEN BRING HIM BACK TO LIFE.

WHEN THE LORDS OF XIBALBA HEAR OF THESE BEGGARS WHO CAN DO MAGIC, THEY HAVE THEM BROUGHT BEFORE THEM.

OH, MY LORD!

WE HAVE HEARD A LOT ABOUT YOUR MAGIC. SHOW US WHAT YOU CAN DO! KILL THAT MAN, AND THEN BRING HIM BACK TO LIFE.

SEE, HIS HEART NO LONGER BEATS.

AND NOW YOU SEE HE IS TRULY ALIVE.

OH, MY! WHAT HAPPENED? I FEEL WONDERFUL. JUST AS IF I HAVE BEEN REBORN.

YOU MUST DO IT TO US.

ME FIRST!

THE TWINS KILL BOTH HUN CAME AND VUCUB CAME. BUT THEY DO NOT BRING THEM BACK TO LIFE. AND SO THIS IS HOW THEY FINALLY DEFEAT THE GODS OF THE UNDERWORLD.

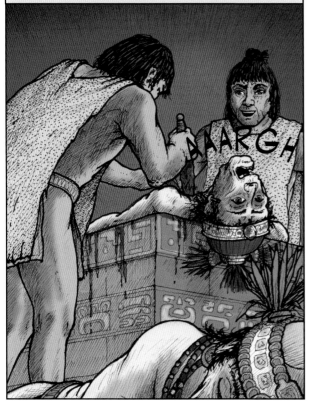

ALL POWER IS TAKEN FROM THE PEOPLE OF XIBALBA, AND THEY ARE REDUCED TO THE LOWEST STATUS AND ARE NEVER ALLOWED TO PLAY BALL AGAIN. NEVER AGAIN WOULD THE KINGDOM OF XIBALBA BE GREAT.

WE ARE HUNAHPU AND XBALANQUE. WE ARE THE SONS OF HUN HUNAHPU.

THEY ARE TOLD OF THE RESTING PLACE OF THEIR FATHER AND UNCLE UNDER THE TLACHTLI-COURT.

THEIR NAMES SHALL NEVER BE FORGOTTEN.

FINALLY, THE TWINS FLOAT INTO THE SKY TO BECOME THE SUN AND THE MOON.   **THE END**

MORE MYTHICAL CHARACTERS

There are thousands of characters in Aztec and Mayan mythology. They include gods and sacred animals, as well as human figures.

BACABS – The Bacabs are the four jaguar gods who hold up the sky. They also guard the four points of the Mayan compass. Each jaguar has its own colour: north is white, south is yellow, west is black and east is red.

CABRACA – Cabraca was an evil Mayan giant who was also called the Mountain Destroyer. He was killed by the Hero Twins.

CAMAZOTZ – This Mayan god of darkness and caves is also known as Zotz or Zotzilaha Chimalman. He is the bat who cut off Hunahpu's head in the story of the Heroic Twins.

CINTEOTL – Cinteotl is the Aztec god of corn, which is the staple diet of the Aztecs. He is often shown wearing a head-dress made from ears of corn and is protected by Tlaloc.

COATLICUE – This Aztec goddess gave birth to the moon and stars. She is usually shown wearing a skirt of snakes woven together, and is known, in particular, as the mother of Huitzilopochtli.

EHÉCATL– Ehécatl is the Aztec god of wind. He brought romantic love into the world when he fell in love with Mayahuel, whom he took from the underworld.

GUCUMATZ – Gucumatz is a Mayan creator god, known as Kukulkán by the Toltecs. He and Omecihuatl try many times to create people. First they use mud, but these people wash away. Then they try wood, but these people do not have a soul. Eventually, they use corn, and this works.

HUITZILOPOCHTLI – This Aztec god of war is thought to be the sun reborn. Huitzilopochtli kills his brothers and sisters (the moon and the stars) as soon as he is born. The fight between them is seen as a fight between day and night.

HURACUN – An important Mayan creator god who is known as the god of storms. The English word 'hurricane' comes from his name.

OMECIHUATL – Omecihuatl is the Aztec goddess of duality because she is two opposites, a man and a woman, at the same time. She gives birth to a stone knife and throws it at Earth to create 1,600 heroes. These heroes create the first people, with help from Xolotl.

TEPEU – A Mayan god of creation who made Earth and everything on it. He, with help from Gucumatz, created it many times because they were not pleased with what they had made.

TLALOC – Tlaloc is the Toltec and Aztec rain god. He is called Chac by the Mayans and rules an Aztec heaven for people who have drowned. He is worshipped because rain allows corn to grow.

XIUHTECUHTLI – This is the Aztec god of fire and time. He is often shown with a red or yellow face. A fire was lit inside the chest of a sacrificed victim once every fifty-two years in his honour.

XOCHIQUETZAL – Xochiquetzal is the goddess of love, beauty, dance, flowers and women. Her name means 'feather flower'. Every year, a feast was held in her honour at which people would wear animal and flower masks.

XOLOTL – An Aztec dog-shaped god, he went to the underworld to find the bones of the first dead humans so he could create more people. Xolotl is Quetzalcóatl's twin brother.

GLOSSARY

arc The curve of the sun's passage across the sky during the day.

bear fruit When a plant blossoms and produces fruit.

blowpipe A tube used mainly for hunting. A hunter would insert a dart into the end of the pipe and blow hard into the opposite end to fire the dart.

calabash A thorny tree common in Mexico and Central America.

coati A type of racoon from Mexico and Central America.

crossroad The point where two or more roads meet each other.

decapitated When someone has had their head cut off.

descendants People who can trace their roots from a particular individual or group.

divert To change the way in which something is travelling.

downfall When a civilisation is defeated.

gourd A fruit with a hard shell, such as a pumpkin, that has been hollowed out and dried.

haste To do something quickly and in a hurry.

jaguar A big cat with a deep yellow coat marked with dark rings, spots or rosettes.

macaw A type of parrot found in Central America.

outwit To succeed by the use of skill and cunning.

Popol Vuh A sacred book of the Mayan people.

rafters The beams that support a sloping roof.

ravines Small narrow tracks with very steep sides that have been created by water running quickly through them.

sacrifice When a person is killed to honour the gods.

sap A liquid that carries food and important substances inside a plant. It is often sticky, such as the sap from the maple tree that is eaten as maple syrup.

soot A black powder that is made by burning something.

status A level of authority.

tlachtli The sacred ball game played by the Mesoamericans.

trickery Playing against another person unfairly and cheating in order to win.

zompopos A species of leaf-cutting ant that is very common in Guatemala, Central America.

For More Information

ORGANISATIONS

The British Museum
Great Russell Street
London
WC1B 3DG
www.thebritishmuseum.ac.uk

FOR FURTHER READING

If you liked this book, you might also want to try:

Avoid becoming an Aztec Sacrifice!
by Fiona Macdonald, Book House 2002

Aztec and Maya Myths
by Karl Taube, British Museum Press 1993

How to be an Aztec Warrior
by Fiona Macdonald, Book House 2005

Tales of the Plumed Serpent: Aztec, Inca and Maya Myths
by Diane Ferguson, Collins and Brown 2000

Inca Myths
by Gary Urton, British Museum Press 1999

The Mythology of Mexico and Central America
by John Bierhorst, Harper Collins 1990

INDEX

Web Sites

Due to the changing nature of Internet links, the Salariya Book Company has developed an online list of Web sites related to the subject of this book. This site is updated regularly. Please use this link to access the list:

http://www.book-house.co.uk/gmyth/azmay